# PLANET EARTH

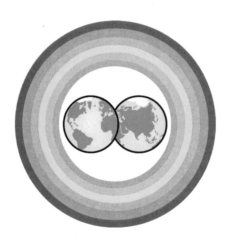

KINGFISHER

NEW YORK

**KINGFISHER**
LONDON & NEW YORK

Text and design copyright © Toucan Books Ltd. 2010
Based on an original concept by Toucan Books Ltd.
Illustrations copyright © Simon Basher 2010

Published in the United States by Kingfisher,
175 Fifth Ave., New York, NY 10010
Kingfisher is an imprint of Pan Macmillan, London.
All rights reserved.

Consultant: Douglas Palmer
Series consultant: Dan Green

Designed and created by Basher
www.basherbooks.com

Dedicated to Claire Rollet

Distributed in the U.S. and Canada by Macmillan, 175 Fifth Ave.,
New York, NY 10010

Library of Congress Cataloging-in-Publication data has been applied for.

ISBN: 978-0-7534-6412-0

Kingfisher books are available for special promotions and premiums.
For details contact: Special Markets Department, Macmillan,
175 Fifth Avenue, New York, NY 10010.

For more information, please visit www.kingfisherbooks.com

Printed in China
14
14TR/0619/WKT/(-)/128MA

# CONTENTS

# Introduction
Planet Earth/Eratosthenes

It's a wide, wild world out there. Planet Earth is filled to the bursting point with Rivers, Mountain Ranges, Weather systems, Climate zones, Ocean currents, Biomes, and all kinds of what-have-yous. There's so much to understand about our planet that the mind boggles.

Eratosthenes (276 B.C.–A.D. 195) is an example of the sort of person who wasn't afraid to look at the big picture. Being a down-to-earth kind of guy with worldly ambitions, he decided to measure Earth's girth. Since he didn't have a tape measure long enough, he used his deep-thinking noggin. His method used a good knowledge of geometry, the locations of various cities, and the Sun's position on a certain day of the year. His answer of 24,662 mi. (39,690km) was only about 1 percent off!

With as many as 50 million undiscovered species, there is much left to explore. Even the Moon's surface is better known than many parts of the Deep Sea. You humans should know that you are not Earth's only inhabitants, and people's actions can affect the planet's delicate balances.

# Eratosthenes

# Earth

- ✵ Home sweet home, AKA the world of "terra"
- ✵ The third planet from the Sun, it circles in the habitable zone
- ✵ This all-around hero is 4.6 billion years old and counting

I'm one of a kind. With the perfect conditions for surface liquid Water, I'm the only known planet in the universe that can protect and nurture the thing we call Life.

I'm a big lovable ball of Rock with a crunchy metal Core at my center, like a jawbreaker. The liquid metal part of my Core generates a magnetic field that protects me from the worst of the Sun's radiation. The deep dialog of The Insiders keeps my insides grumbling. My surface is Wet, Wet, Wet. More than two-thirds of it is covered in liquid Water, the life-giving juice that shapes my drier parts—the continental Landlubbers. Next comes a little Atmosphere—a thin layer of air where the Weather Gang hangs out. The thin shell covering my surface is called the biosphere and is home to the Lively Crew. Time to Go Global!

The Moon, circling Earth at 238,900 mi., is its only natural satellite.

- ● Distance from Sun: 93 million mi.
- ● Surface area: 196.9 million sq. mi.
- ● Earth's tilt: 23.5°

Earth

# CHAPTER 1

## The Insiders

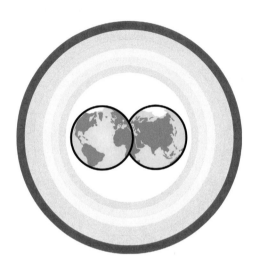

From deep in its belly to its outer layer, The Insiders help make planet Earth what it is—a cut-and-thrust place with a lot going on under the surface. Earth is a warm and mostly solid planet with a 24,850-mi. (40,000-km) waist. Think of Earth as an egg—Core is the yolk, Mantle the white, and Crust the thin shell. But Crust is not all it's cracked up to be—it's made of crazy-paving sections called Plates that drift around over the surface. Their nonstop movements give rise to many a savage Volcano and Earthquake, which judder the planet to the Core.

Core

Mantle

Crust

Plates

Hot Spot

Earthquake

Volcano

Rocks

Minerals

Fossil Fuels

# Core
## ■ The Insiders

※ A superhot heavyweight that sits at the center of Earth
※ Has two parts—the solid inner core and the liquid outer core
※ Currents in its liquid part generate Earth's magnetic field

I'm called the Colonel because I'm right at the heart of things (kernel—get it?). I look like a giant shiny metal ball bearing. With all my iron content (I'm mostly iron, together with a tiny bit of nickel), I take the credit for making planet Earth a giant magnet.

When it comes to structure, I'm a bit like an inside-out chocolate truffle—crunchy on the inside but liquid on the outside. It's hot, hot, hot being stuck in the middle of a planet—hot enough to melt metal—but the insane pressures at the center of Earth cause my inner parts to stay solid. You might call me dense, but don't take me lightly. I'm an extremely weighty character. Although I make up only about one-sixth of Earth's volume, I account for almost one-third of its mass.

Earth's magnetic field changes its direction every 200,000 years.

● Temperature: up to 12,600°F
● Diameter: 2,166 mi.
● Mass of Core: 2.166 billion trillion tons

Core

# Mantle

## ■ The Insiders

* ✳ A big thicky that sits between Crust and Core
* ✳ Almost five-sixths of Earth's volume and two-thirds of its mass
* ✳ Convection forces push Plates around on Earth's surface

Most people forget about me. When they think of Earth, they imagine Crust with all its fancy mountains and playful Oceans or the mysterious metal Core. Well, I may be a bulky, laid-back kind of fellow who oozes, slothlike, under the surface, but I've got Core surrounded on all sides, and I can tear Crust apart with the merest shrug.

Although I'm mostly solid as a Rock, when I get hot under the collar, I can turn into fiery hot liquid Rock (called magma). Just beneath Crust my temperature is an oozing 900–1,650°F (500–900°C), but at the edge of Core I'm around 7,200°F (4000°C) and totally solid. Although I stay calm deep inside, I move Plates around on Earth's surface, causing Earthquakes and Volcanoes. It's the huge plumes of hot magma rising from my depths that create Hot Spots.

Mantle gets solid because its melting point rises as its pressure increases.

* ● Temperature: 900–7,200°F
* ● Thickness: 1,800 mi.
* ● Mass of Mantle: 4.393 billion trillion tons

## Mantle

# Crust

## ■ The Insiders

- ✴ Our planet's beautiful, richly colored surface
- ✴ Made of the solid Rock of the Continents and the seabed
- ✴ Crusty by name, crusty by nature . . . it's The Insiders' fragile guy!

Beauty is skin deep, but that's fine with me—I've got all the looks! While Core and Mantle may be hot stuff, I'm the face of Earth and the one with all the scenery. Some may point out that I'm just solidified scum that floated to the surface when Earth was young and molten, but we all know that yummy cream rises to the top.

I'm thicker in some parts than others. Just like a reflection in a crystal-clear Lake, the shapes I form at the surface are mirrored below. So, beneath Mountain Ranges, huge "antiranges" poke down into Mantle. Basalt lies under most of the Oceans, and granite forms the bread and butter of the Continents. On top of this there is a thin scraping of sedimentary Rock, made mostly from ground-up pieces of igneous Rock and dead organisms.

Crust makes up less than 1 percent of Earth's volume.

- ● Maximum thickness: 56 mi.
- ● Minimum thickness: 2.5 mi.
- ● Most common Rock in Crust: basalt

Crust

# Plates

## ■ The Insiders

✴ Plates move apart, crash, and slide alongside one another
✴ Shifting Plates can make Oceans widen or disappear altogether
✴ The science of Plates is called plate tectonics

Think the ground beneath your feet is going nowhere? Think again! Crust is not as fixed as he looks at first glance. More like a hard-boiled egg with a broken shell, he's made up of pieces called Plates that are slowly on the move.

My crew floats on Mantle and slides very slowly over Earth's surface with the cooler, denser Plates slipping down into Mantle. Where we're moving apart, new Crust is being made to fill in the gaps, and where we're crushing together, old Crust gets pushed back into hot Mantle. All this jostling of stubborn Rock causes Earthquakes. Plates fit together snugly like pieces in a jigsaw puzzle—if you look at the shape of the eastern coast of South America and the western coast of Africa, you can see where two Plates once rubbed side by side.

Plates move at about the same speed that fingernails grow.

● Total number: 8 main Plates
● Biggest Plate: Pacific Plate
● Smallest Plate: Juan de Fuca Plate, U.S.

16

Plates

# Hot Spot

## ■ The Insiders

- ☀ A point at Earth's surface where Mantle is superhot
- ☀ Causes Volcanoes, geysers, and other steamy stuff
- ☀ Supervolcanoes are the biggest natural threat to humankind

Hot diggity dog! Things get steamy when I'm around. You don't want to hang around too long—before you know it, the ground will be hissing with gas, bubbling up with superheated Water, and spitting fire and Rock out of Earth. Like a huge, angry pimple on Earth's face, I'm fed from below by a rising column of sizzling, gooey magma.

I appear whenever scorching magma rises up from deep within Mantle, creating enormous Volcanoes. The molten liquid begins to melt Crust before it explodes out onto Earth's surface as lava. The islands of Hawaii were my creation. A Hot Spot under Yellowstone National Park has the potential to form a mega-destructive supervolcano! I'm still shrouded in mystery, though— no one knows much about how I form.

John Tuzo Wilson came up with the term *hot spot* in 1963.

- ● Major Ocean Hot Spot: Hawaii
- ● Major land Hot Spot: Iceland
- ● Number of identified Hot Spot areas: 50

Hot Spot

# Earthquake

## ■ The Insiders

☀ A release of energy from Rocks, making the ground tremble
☀ Kick-started by movements of Earth's Plates and Volcanoes
☀ Most common where plates crash or slide past each other

I shake things up. Everything trembles before my mighty power—mountains, Oceans, forests, skyscrapers, and highways. I can be dangerous and destructive, but I can't help it. Pressure just builds up, and then I explode.

Earth's Plates don't just move smoothly—they are always squeezing past or pushing against each other. With all the pressure that keeps piling up behind these vast masses of Rock, friction between them can stop them only for a bit. When their sticking points come unstuck, I am let loose with a sudden and often violent release of energy. My shock waves cause the ground to quake. Powerful quakes heave Plates all over the place. Quakes on the Ocean floor can set off giant waves called tsunamis, which travel at great speeds and can cause destruction.

Earthquakes are measured on the Richter scale from 1 to 10.

● Major Earthquake zone: circum-Pacific belt
● Most Earthquake-prone country: Japan
● Largest: Chile, May 22, 1960 (8.5)

Earthquake

# Volcano

## ■ The Insiders

- ✳ A blister in Crust that is formed from rising molten Rock
- ✳ Normally found in clusters or strings on Earth's surface
- ✳ Can be dormant (quiet) for centuries between eruptions

Go on, call me a pimple if you dare! When I'm in a foul mood, it's time for the scientists to leave the area and let all their probing gizmos monitor my temperature. I'm deadly—the vapors that I spurt can poison whole towns.

Some say I'm like a big zit. Well, yeah, I do break out on Earth's surface, fill up with angry liquid, and grow until I erupt. I'm famous for spewing oozy lava, erupting sky high with columns of ash, throwing boiling clouds of dust and mud down my sides, and chucking out a medley of Rock bombs. When I'm feeling most menacing, I can blow my top. I'm most likely to appear in places where Plates join. I had my heyday four billion years ago, when I played a big, friendly part in cooling the molten planet—the gases I released back then formed the early Atmosphere.

Cinder cones and lava domes are the most common types of Volcanoes.

- ● Largest Volcano: Mauna Loa, Hawaii
- ● Most deadly eruption: Tambora (1815)
- ● Number of eruptions every year: 50–60

Volcano

# Rocks

## ■ The Insiders

* ☀ Tough customers that make up the ground we walk on
* ☀ Three of a kind—pick one as your favorite Rock star
* ☀ Rocks are rock hard, but igneous Rocks were once big softies

We are the hard stuff that Crust is made of. We come in three types: Igneous Rocks form from molten magma, lava, and ash that have cooled. Sedimentary Rocks are built up of many layers of sediment over long periods. Metamorphic Rocks are made when sedimentary or igneous Rocks get heated and squeezed until they morph (change) into weird and wonderful new types.

Rocks

The Rock feldspar makes up 60 percent of Earth's crust.

* ● Common sedimentary: limestone, shale
* ● Common igneous: basalt, granite
* ● Common metamorphic: slate, marble

※ These solid little characters live in the ground
※ Some are solitary types, but others gather together in Rocks
※ Mineral ores may be heated to extract valuable metals

Minerals

We are the things that make Rocks what they are. Without us, they are nothing! There are rules for being in our gang— you need a predictable chemical composition and a definite internal structure. Rocks may vary, but we do not waver! In our clan are metals and some of the world's most valuable and beautiful crystals, plus many that are common as mud!

● Most common mineral: quartz
● Most valuable mineral: diamond
● World's largest crystal: gypsum (55 tons)

The Golden Jubilee (545.67 carats) is the world's largest cut diamond.

# Fossil Fuels

## ■ The Insiders

✴ The three amigos of power production—coal, oil, and gas
✴ Energy providers made from ancient living things
✴ Burned in power plants, they also create greenhouse gases

We're old. Some say we're dirty fuels because we're not renewable like Tide and Wind. But you need us for electricity to power essentials such as heating and cooking.

Coal, oil, and gas were all formed from living things that died and were buried deep in Earth. Coal was once plant material from ancient swamps. Oil was squashed from the bodies of tiny sea creatures. Gas is burped up as coal and oil are squeezed and heated inside Earth. The energy that was stored by these prehistoric life forms when they were alive is released when we Fossil Fuels are burned. In most places we are mined and drilled from far underground, but sometimes we have moved naturally up to the surface. Oil can be refined to make sparkier fuels such as gasoline, diesel, and aviation fuel.

Fossil fuels provide about 85 percent of our energy demands.

● Coal buried: 354–15 million years ago
● Density of crude oil: less than Water
● Main chemical in natural gas: methane

Fossil Fuels

# CHAPTER 2
## Going Global

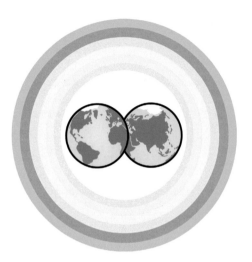

When it comes to Earth's surface, this hard-working crew has got it covered. Between them they divvy up the globe and make it measurable. They pinpoint exactly where things are, allowing people to measure distances, make maps, and navigate. Like a net cast over Earth, they are the foundation of the Global Positioning System (GPS). Although they are mighty useful, each Going Global crew member exists only as a concept to help make Earth more understandable to us. So, if you travel to the equator, you won't really find a hoop that circles the planet!

Longitude

Latitude

Equator

Tropics

Poles

# Longitude
## ■ Going Global

※ This long fellow divides Earth up into 24 vertical segments
※ Helps calculate distance traveled around Earth
※ Measured in degrees and minutes, east and west

I am a straight-up kind of guy. My lines carve up the planet like segments of an orange, cutting through the lines of Latitude at right angles. None of my lines cross, but they all meet at the North and South poles. The line that runs through Greenwich, England, is called the prime meridian and is set at zero degrees. East of the prime meridian, clocks jump forward. Travel west and they lag behind.

Longitude

First accurately measured by Englishman John Harrison in 1737.

● Longitude of London, England: 0° 5' W
● Longitude of New York City: 73° 58' W
● Longitude of Sydney, Australia: 151° 17' E

# Latitude

## Going Global

* This striped guy divides Earth up into five horizontal zones
* Marks out Earth's chilly, temperate, and hot Climate zones
* Measured in degrees and minutes, north and south

Latitude

I am the planet's greatest all-arounder. My horizontal lines hug Earth, forming big hoops around the globe. My longest, most famous line is Equator, but I have four significant others. Between sweltering-hot Tropics and the Arctic and Antarctic circles, there are the temperate zones. In hand with Longitude, I let you pinpoint your location with devastating accuracy. Give me some (L)attitude!

* Latitude of London, England: 51° 32' N
* Latitude of New York City: 40° 47' N
* Latitude of Sydney, Australia: 33° 55' S

Major lines are the Arctic Circle, Antarctic Circle, Tropics, and Equator.

# Equator
## ■ Going Global

* This even-handed character circles Earth's middle
* Farther from the Poles than any other line of Latitude
* Splits Earth into Northern and Southern hemispheres

As the longest and most important line of Latitude in the whole wide world, it would be easy for me to become bigheaded. But it's not in my nature. I am an even splitter—the equator—who girdles the planet like a big belt. When it comes to taking sides between north and south, I don't just sit on the fence—I am the fence!

Slap bang on the world's hottest, steamiest parts, I am roasty toasty. I might be just a line, but I am a significant divider. My path is often painted on the ground so that people can have the pleasure of putting a foot in both hemispheres at the same time. At sea, sailors sometimes have a ceremony when they first cross me. I have even given my name to two countries: Ecuador, which I run through, and Equatorial Guinea, which is not far from me.

Earth is not a perfect sphere but bulges around the Equator.

● Latitude: 0° N/S
● Length: 24,901.5 mi.
● Number of countries crossed: 13

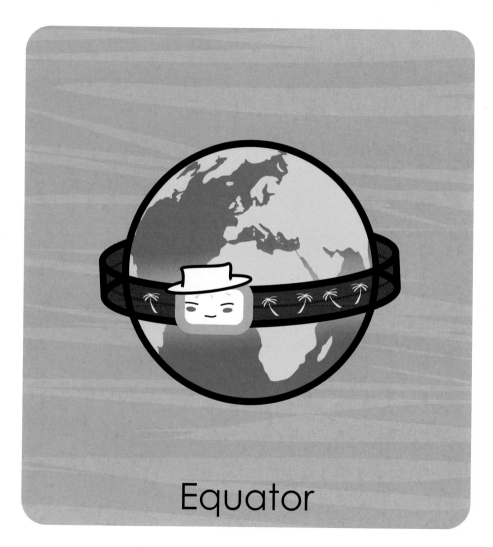

Equator

# Tropics
## ■ Going Global

✳ Terrible twins called Cancer and Capricorn
✳ Lines of Latitude sandwiching Earth's sweaty regions
✳ Share the name *Tropics* with the region they contain

Step inside the sweatbox! If you can't stand the heat, you'd better stay clear of us. We're a tropical twosome who run around the globe at equal distances north and south of Equator (23° 26', if you must know).

The northerly twin is the Tropic of Cancer, and the southerly one is the Tropic of Capricorn. We're so special that we appear as dotted lines of Latitude on maps of the world. In between us is the humid and sticky region called the tropics, and the world's hot Deserts. Because Earth's tilt is not so great here, the Sun shines directly overhead for most of the year—its energy takes the most direct route through the Atmosphere and hits the ground with its full force. The Tropics has only two Seasons—dry and rainy—so it switches from baking hot to drenching monsoon.

Cancer crosses 18 countries and Capricorn 11 countries.

● Latitude of Cancer: 23° 26' N
● Latitude of Capricorn: 23° 26' S
● Distance between Tropics: 3,000 mi.

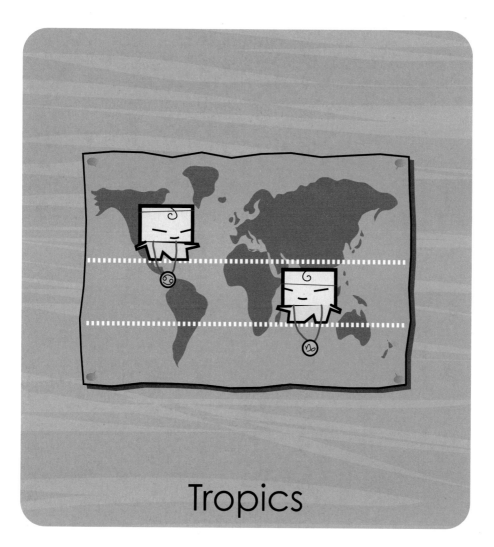

# Tropics

# Poles

## ■ Going Global

- ✹ Pair of Arctic and Antarctic monkeys who are polar opposites
- ✹ World-famous double act of cold, icy extremes
- ✹ Desolate circles visited only by explorers and adventurers

We're two of a kind, but we're poles apart. Sitting on top of the world (depending on your way of looking at things!), we Poles are at the most northern and southern tips of the planet. North Pole is the one with no land (just ice) whereas South Pole is on the continent of Antarctica.

The regions inside the Arctic Circle (north) and Antarctic Circle (south) are called the polar regions. We are home to lots of ice and snow—and the odd hungry beast.  Of course, you won't actually find a pole at either Pole. Like all our Going Global buddies, we're points on the map rather than real, solid objects. Because compasses point to the magnetic Poles—which aren't quite centered on the geographical Pole and have a tricky habit of moving around year by year—we Poles are fixed at 90° latitude.

Polar bears live near the North Pole and penguins near the South Pole.

- ● First man to N. Pole: R.E. Peary (1909)
- ● First man to S. Pole: R. Amundsen (1911)
- ● Coldest: South Pole (−117°F, 1978)

Poles

# CHAPTER 3
## Landlubbers

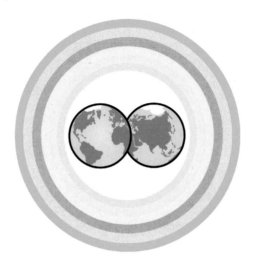

This group forms the ground you walk on. Together they make up some of the most visible features on Earth's face. Most of them can be seen from space, and the largest, Continents, can be seen from the Moon. The world's Mountain Ranges form natural barriers, separating animals and people alike. They also affect Weather, causing Clouds to form and Precipitation to fall. To us, their peaks seem enormous, but compared with Earth itself, they are minute. If our planet were small enough to hold in one hand, it would feel as smooth as a billiard ball.

Continents

Mountain Range

Plateaus

Rift Valley

Peninsula

Island

Coast

# Continents

## Landlubbers

* These lumbering lumps are the biggest landmasses on Earth
* Together they make up almost all the land on the planet
* They have a couple of loners, but most stick together

We are the Magnificent Seven—North America, South America, Antarctica, Africa, Europe, Asia, and Australia. (But some geographers are still arguing that there are only six because Europe and Asia sit shoulder to shoulder, divided only by the mighty Ural Mountains.) Proud, hulking hunks of Rock, we—with the exception of chilly Antarctica—play host to your puny race. We are chock-full of goodies that you can dig out and use to keep you fed, manufacture things, and power your machines.

We've been around for about four billion years, trundling here and there around the surface, jostled by Plates. By now we should have separated from one another, but some of us are still joined together by sneaky little fingers of land—just look at North and South America.

Europe, North America, and South America would all fit inside Asia!

* Biggest: Asia (16,915,353 sq. mi.)
* Smallest: Australia (2,941,298 sq. mi.)
* Most populated: Asia

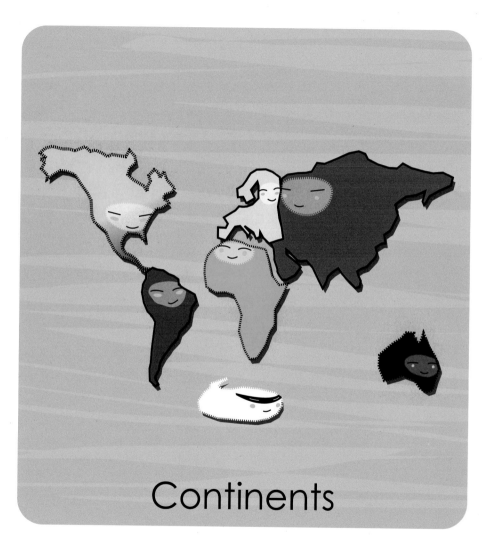

# Continents

# Mountain Range

## ■ Landlubbers

✳ Landform that stands head and shoulders above the rest
✳ This down-to-earth guy is the crumple zone of crashed Plates
✳ A monster who divides Continents and give rise to Rivers

Distant, magical, cold, and inaccessible, I am a lofty fellow whose head is in the Clouds. People can't help looking up to me, and they have made me the mythical seat of demons and dragons. But the truth is more unbelievable!

I snake across the land in belts and chains, like scars on Continents. These lines are the stitch marks where two bits of Earth's Crust have been forcibly joined together as Plates collide. The mighty whoomph of Plates crumpling into one another pushes Crust up in huge wrinkles that form my longest ranges. The taller and more jagged my peaks, the younger I am, because older ranges have been worn down and smoothed by Erosion. The Himalaya mountain range is still on the up and up. Every year, as the Indian Plate piles into Asia, it rises by 0.4 in. (1cm).

Mount McKinley, at 20,320 ft., is the highest mountain in North America.

● Highest: Himalayas, Asia (29,029 ft.)
● Longest: Andes, S. America (5,600 mi.)
● Fastest-growing: Himalayas

# Mountain Range

# Plateaus

## ■ Landlubbers

- ✳ A flattop crew of high standers who are held in high regard
- ✳ Some stand alone; others are stuck between mountains
- ✳ They're home to many of Earth's unique plants and animals

Stand tall and be counted is our motto. Although we are pretty high and mighty, we're a levelheaded bunch who are much less spiky than those showoff Mountain Ranges.

To join our club, you need to tower at least 1,500 ft. (457m) above sea level, have at least one steep side, and have a flattish top. It doesn't matter how much area you cover— just a few square miles will do—but our more distinguished members are larger than some whole countries. There are a few different types in our club: those made at the same time as Mountain Ranges; those formed from very old bits of Crust lifted up high; and those cast from the eroded remains of vast lava flows. Over long periods of isolation, cut off from the surrounding land by cliffs or mountains, we have evolved many specialized forms of plant life.

Plateaus are also called tablelands.

- ● Largest: Tibetan Plateau (965,255 sq. mi.)
- ● Highest: Tibetan Plateau (14,800 ft.)
- ● Most famous: Table Mountain, S. Africa

Plateaus

# Rift Valley
## Landlubbers

* Deep chasm caused by Crust pulling itself apart
* Biggest are on the seabed, but there are giant ones on land
* Hotbed of activity, with Volcanoes and steaming springs

One of the world's biggest holes in the ground, I am the pits! As an enormous stretch mark on a Continent, I show where Earth's mighty Plates are pulling apart.

As the ground stretches and strains, Crust becomes thin and flattened out like pizza dough. Eventually, it slips downward, making my characteristic flat valley floor with its very steep sidewalls. Here Crust is so thin that Volcanoes and a lot of other hot stuff spring up. My valley bottom often floods, creating long Lakes. I'm most famous as Africa's Great Rift Valley. Along its length are some of the world's biggest Lakes as well as the source of the Nile River. But the daddy of all Rift Valleys runs unseen and underwater, forming a seam that runs the entire length of the Atlantic Ocean.

The Baikal Rift Zone in Siberia has the world's deepest lake (2.2 mi.).

* Length of Great Rift Valley: 3,700 mi.
* Countries crossed by Great Rift Valley: 15
* Longest: Mid-Atlantic Ridge (8,700 mi.)

Rift Valley

# Peninsula

## ■ Landlubbers

* Sticks out from a shoreline like a sore thumb
* Watching its figure, it is never as fat as it is tall
* Likes variety and appears in all shapes and sizes

I'm all fingers and thumbs. No matter what I do, I always seem to stick out. I never asked to be noticed, but I can't help it. Almost completely surrounded by Water, but never quite cut off, I jut out from Islands and Continents. I have to be longer than I am wide. Crucially, I keep myself grounded—I'm well connected and always linked to dry land.

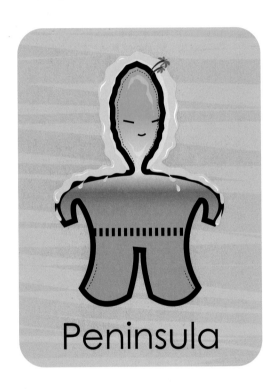

Peninsula

It can carry whole countries—for example Spain and Portugal.

● World's largest: Arabian Peninsula
● Europe's largest: Scandinavian Peninsula
● North America's largest: Alaska

# Island

## Landlubbers ■

- ✷ An independent character who goes it alone
- ✷ Found in bodies of Water, from Oceans to ponds
- ✷ Sometimes gangs up with others to make an archipelago

Island

Give me some space! Surrounded by Water, I prefer to stand alone in splendid isolation. I can be big, like Madagascar, or a tiny dot of Rock, like Bishop Rock in the U.K. (the world's smallest). It doesn't matter, as long as I'm separated from any mainland by a decent-size body of Water. Canals and Rivers don't count, or else much of Brazil and Venezuela would be Islands, too!

- ● Biggest: Greenland (840,000 sq. mi.)
- ● 8th biggest: Great Britain (88,753 sq. mi.)
- ● Biggest archipelago: 17,000 Islands

A group of Islands is called an archipelago (say "arky-pella-go").

# Coast

## ■ Landlubbers

✳ The steadfast defender of the land
✳ A complex type with a character that's full of twists and turns
✳ Looks solid enough, but its shores are always changing

I live life on the brink. At the very edge of the land, I alone hold back the sea, protecting land from the powerful Ocean. Whether you are on the beaches of the Caribbean or the mighty cliffs of Dover, there's simply no farther you can go without getting your feet wet!

I'm a tough cookie, but Ocean grinds me down. I'm riddled with nicks, notches, and indentations, where the waves have beaten me back. Here I form coves, bays, and beaches. I play host to the mouths of Rivers as they spill into the sea, and where the waters mix, you will often find estuaries and Deltas. In Norway, my edges are deeply scored by long inlets known as fjords. These are valleys cut by Glaciers, which are then flooded by the sea. But my most impressive features are my jutting cliffs.

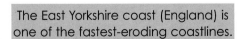
The East Yorkshire coast (England) is one of the fastest-eroding coastlines.

● Length of U.S. coastline: 12,380 mi.
● Length of world's coastline: 313,200 mi.
● Highest cliff: Kalaupapa, Hawaii (3,300 ft.)

# Coast

# CHAPTER 4
## Wet! Wet! Wet!

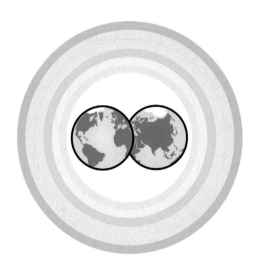

Planet Earth is a big baby-blue ball of wetness. For starters, water covers 71 percent of Earth's surface—that's more than twice as much as dry land. But "dry land" isn't really dry—it's dotted with Lakes and Rivers, plus when rain falls, the whole group gets even wetter. This soggy bunch form Earth's defining feature, because they make it unique among all the bodies circling the Sun. Without them, life could not exist. River, Ocean, Glacier, and Erosion are always reshaping the landscape, sometimes dramatically (depending on their mood!). This world belongs to Water.

Water

River

Delta

Lake

Ocean

Tide

Glacier

Icecap

Erosion

# Water

## Wet! Wet! Wet!

* A wet and wild "hydro" guy who is central to planet Earth
* Earth is the solar system's only planet with surface Water
* Life would not have evolved without the help of this guy

Yep. I'm a big wet one . . . yada, yada. I am the most essential substance on this planet and cover 71 percent of Earth's surface. Life as we know it is simply not possible without me. I make up 70 percent of every human being. But all these figures are water off a duck's back to me!

You can find me in three very different guises. My most common form is as liquid Water, flowing in Rivers and filling up Crust's low points as Lakes and Oceans. But I'm not always gushing. I turn solid when I freeze and make up the Icecaps and Glaciers, plus the sheets of ice that form on Lakes and Rivers when it's well below 32°F (0°C). My ghostly form is as an invisible gaseous water vapor, which fills up the Atmosphere with billowing Clouds before falling from the sky as rain, hail, and snow.

Earth's total supply of Water is 326.28 million cu. mi. (1.36 billion km³).

● Melting point: 32°F
● Boiling point: 212°F
● Chemical symbol: $H_2O$

Water

# River
## Wet! Wet! Wet!

☀ The only way is downhill for this freshwater fellow
☀ Its long and winding antics erode and shape the land
☀ A major sediment transporter who ends up in Oceans or Lakes

My life starts out on a high as a young and sprightly mover. Fed by rainfall, I trickle down Rocks before speeding up as I rumble over waterfalls and down to the valley floor. By this time I'm swollen with Water from all the smaller rivulets that have joined me on the way. I meander around in wide loops until I spill out into the sea at my mouth. Here, my job as a transporter ends.

River

Angel Falls in Venezuela is the largest waterfall, at 3,212 ft. (979m) high.

● Longest: Nile (4,258 mi.)
● Largest: Amazon Basin (2.7 million sq. mi.)
● Amount of Earth's Water in Rivers: 0.0001%

# Delta

## Wet! Wet! Wet!

* ✳ Found on the muddiest, most foul-mouthed Rivers
* ✳ Made up of muddy Islands and small channels of Water
* ✳ Has two main shapes: arcuate (triangular) and bird's foot

Delta

Sluggish and tangled, I clog up River mouths with a mess of mud and tiny channels. I form soft, squishy land. I'm a hodgepodge, but it's not really my fault. I'm built from the sludgy sediment that big, brown, muddy Rivers carry down to the sea with them. I am born when Rivers flow too lethargically to carry their sandy, silty load out to sea and when the sea is too slack to wash this away.

* ● Largest: Ganges Delta (40,540 sq. mi.)
* ● Arcuate examples: Nile Delta; Niger Delta
* ● Bird's foot example: Mississippi Delta

The Pearl River Delta in China has the most complex pattern.

# Lake
## ■ Wet! Wet! Wet!

☀ A large body of Water enclosed on all sides by land
☀ A squishy-bottomed fellow fed by Rivers and streams
☀ Usually filled with fresh Water, but some are salty

Serene and calm, I'm a watery fellow who prefers peace and quiet. Sometimes Wind stirs me up, but I'm an unruffled type who is generally not bothered by that troublesome Tide. I like to lie low in Earth's hollows and nooks, surrounded on all sides by land. Sometimes I'm even found in large underground wells called aquifers, which are tapped to provide lovely, fresh drinking Water.

I'm kept full by streams and rainy runoff, and I drain out into Rivers. This cycle generally keeps my Water fresh. But if the Sun evaporates my Water and leaves behind all the dissolved salts and other Minerals, I can become brackish (salty). Earth's saltiest Water body, the Dead Sea, is a lake. My watery pools are unique to Earth, but on Saturn's moon Titan, the Lakes are made of alien, undrinkable ethane!

Lake Superior is the largest freshwater Lake, at 31,700 sq. mi. ( 82,100km$^2$).

● Largest area: Caspian Sea (143,000 sq. mi.)
● Largest volume: Lake Baikal (5,700 cu. mi.)
● Deepest: Lake Baikal (5,315 ft.)

Lake

# Ocean
## Wet! Wet! Wet!

* This watery monster covers 66 percent of Earth's surface
* It contains 97 percent of all the world's Water
* A global geezer that is split into five parts by geographers

You call your world Earth, but I'm the biggest single surface feature. Continents with their Rivers, Lakes, mountains, and Deserts get all the glory, even though I'm the one who covers almost three-fourths of the planet and has trenches that are deeper than land's mountains. No wonder Earth is also known as the Blue Planet.

Look at any world map and you'll see that I'm one mighty global Ocean, but people split me into five separate parts: the Atlantic, Pacific, Indian, Arctic, and Southern oceans. I'm known for my stormy temper, which raises Hurricanes and cyclones, but I'm important to Earth. I regulate global temperatures, Climate, and Wind patterns, and I'm a big source for Precipitation. For more than three billion years, all Life called me home, before some crawled onto land.

Water pressure in the deep parts of the ocean would crush any human!

* Largest: Pacific Ocean (69.5 sq. mi.)
* Smallest: Arctic Ocean (5.4 million sq. mi.)
* Deepest: Pacific Ocean (35,830 ft.)

Ocean

# Tide

## Wet! Wet! Wet!

- ✳ A changeable fellow who spends his time going in and out
- ✳ A truly global phenomenon that happens twice a day
- ✳ A child of the Moon, despite being stuck down here on Earth

My life is full of ups and downs. I am a seesaw kind of guy who is always being pulled up by the Moon while the rest of me drops down. I'm most visible on the Coast, but it's often hard to see whether I'm coming or going!

I owe my power over the world's Oceans to the Moon. The pull of its gravity drags water toward it. I am always highest on the part of Earth facing the Moon, where the Moon is directly overhead, and on the opposite side of the planet. I am lowest exactly between these two places. Earth is always spinning, so the part facing the Moon changes throughout the day. That is why I rise and fall. When the Moon and Sun are on the same side of Earth, their gravitational pull doubles up my highest highs, causing spring tides. My lowest lows are called neap tides.

The Mediterranean and Caribbean seas have almost no tidal range.

- ● World's greatest daily tidal range: 55 ft. (Bay of Fundy, Canada)
- ● World's lowest daily tidal range: 8 in.

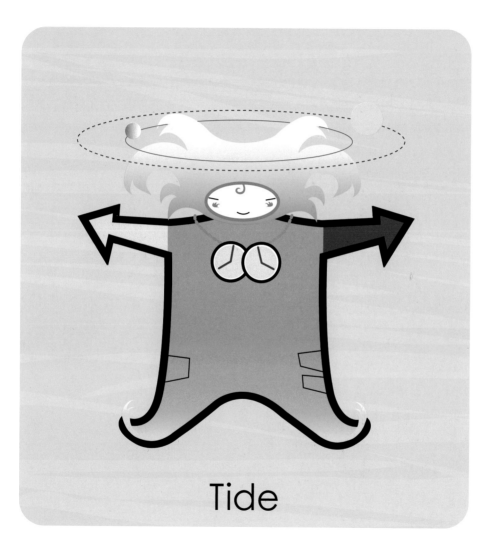

Tide

# Glacier

## Wet! Wet! Wet!

✳ This icy powerhouse is rugged, but a bit of a slow mover
✳ Carves distinctive U-shaped valleys, filled with crevices
✳ It is beating a fast retreat in some parts of the world

Craggy and cold, I'm the old man of the mountains. I'm a feature of most mountains that have year-round snow. When snowfall builds up and compacts into ice, I'm born and start to crawl slowly down the mountainside. My great weight grinds away Rock beneath me, and bits break off. I finish when I get far enough downhill to melt, and my snout gives rise to meltwater streams.

Glacier

If all the world's Glaciers melted, the Ocean would rise by 230 ft. (70m).

● Longest: Lambert-Fisher (320 mi.)
● Longest in N. America: Bering (118 mi.)
● Fastest-moving: 367 ft. per day

# Icecap

## Wet! Wet! Wet! ■

* ☀ This frosty character keeps a cool lid on things
* ☀ Melts a bit every summer but regrows again in the winter
* ☀ Global warming is causing both Icecaps to get smaller

Icecap

Sitting chilly over the Poles and Greenland, I'm an icy fellow who gives visitors the cold shoulder. I'm definitely not the kind of cap you'd want to put on your head! My frozen wastes cover both land and sea, keeping Water locked up in an icy blanket. But things are changing. As temperatures on Earth climb and I melt, the Oceans rise and turn into a ticking time bomb.

* ● Biggest: Antarctic (5.4 million sq. mi.)
* ● Thickest: Antarctic (up to 2 mi.)
* ● Arctic ice lost since 1978: 20 percent

Icecaps hold more than 98 percent of Earth's fresh water.

# Erosion
## Wet! Wet! Wet!

* This guy tears down Mountain Ranges
* Water's best pal, the two of them are virtually inseparable
* A force to be reckoned with, it loves to shape land

Come and have a go if you think you're hard enough! It doesn't matter how tough you are—I will wear you down. I am the force that grinds mountains to dust. Big-bruiser Rocks tremble at the mention of my name.

Water and Wind do most of my heavy work. Ocean waves ceaselessly pound and wear away coastlines, while Rivers and Glaciers sculpt land by rubbing and carving it. Rain just ekes away at everything, carrying soil and Rock away grain by grain. Frost is the cold sore of Erosion as it penetrates cracks in Rocks and smashes them to smithereens from the inside. When it comes to wearing things away, I like to take my time. I am slow, I admit—too slow for most people to notice—but I get the job done. Nowhere is spared. I'm taking you down!

Arches, canyons, and caves are all Erosion's handiwork.

● Quick to erode: limestone, mudstone
● Slow to erode: granite, basalt, marble
● Fastest coastal Erosion: U.K. (6.5 ft. per year)

Erosion

# CHAPTER 5
## Weather Gang

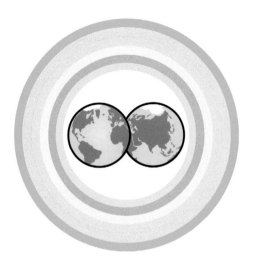

People love chatting about this quirky group (especially if there's something to complain about!). They're a fickle bunch who rule our lives and have a habit of raining on our parade! You can't count on the weather forecast, as these characters enjoy keeping us guessing. Why are they so hard to pin down? You'll soon find out. From that naughty El Niño kid in the Pacific Ocean to the head-banging tussles of Fronts in the skies above us, there are a million things that make the Weather what it is. No wonder nobody really knows "whether" it's going to rain or shine!

Weather

Climate

Atmosphere

Front

Seasons

Sunshine

Water Cycle

Precipitation

Cloud

Wind

Hurricane

Drought

Flood

El Niño

Greenhouse Effect

Climate Change

# Weather

## Weather Gang

* This changeable character blows hot and cold
* Best remembered for his stormy temper and bad behavior
* His partnership with Erosion makes for an Earth-shaping force

Catch me if you can. I am one of the least predictable of Earth's many characters—a real four-seasons-in-one-day type. Everything is temporary for me. I live for the minute, and although meteorologists (weather scientists) try to forecast my mood swings, I often give them the old slippery slip and do something quite unexpected!

My best tricks are well known—Cloud, rain, Wind, snow, fog, storms, and Sunshine. Just look at all my Weather symbols! But when things get out of control, I also have natural disasters up my sleeve, such as Hurricanes, Droughts, Floods, and global warming. You may look up to me, but I'm not so high and mighty. I occur mainly in the lower Atmosphere, fueled by changing pressures between one part and another.

As much as 36 ft. (11m) of rain per year can fall in parts of India.

● Heat record: Libya, 136.0°F (1922)
● Cold record: Antarctica, −128.9°F (1983)
● Heat record in the U.S.: Calif., 134°F (1913)

# Weather

# Climate

## Weather Gang

- Steady guy who is often confused with Weather
- Predictable and less subject to sudden change than Weather
- Normally measured as an average of Weather over 30 years

I'm the steady, dependable type. I do what I say I'll do, and I don't go changing willy-nilly like that fidget Weather. Wanna know the difference between me and Weather? I'm what you expect; Weather is what you get.

Because I'm a measure of the average Weather that a place receives, I can stay the same for centuries. It's I who determines what kinds of plants grow and what kinds of animals roam any given territory. Instead of depending entirely on Atmosphere, I also count on Latitude, type of terrain, and height above sea level, plus Oceans and their currents. For this reason I exist in zones, where Weather is largely controlled by me. In the Tropics, for example, I make for warm, wet Weather, and in Tundra, I make for dry, cold Weather. You'll understand me monsoon-er or later!

The main climate zones are tropical, monsoon, dry, warm, cool, and cold.

- Hottest 30 years on record: 1970–2000
- $CO_2$ in Atmosphere: 40% more than in 1860
- A climate scientist is called a climatologist

Climate

# Atmosphere

■ Weather Gang

✳ A complex, layered character who is made up of many gases
✳ Separates the surface of planet Earth from space
✳ Life is lived in its lowest, densest layer, the troposphere

Much more than just a lightweight gasbag, I am the big comfort blanket around Earth that protects Life. I soak up all the nasty stuff (like Sun's deadly radiation), trap heat to keep things cozy, and smooth out chilly extremes. Weather plays around in the troposphere. Above, the ozone layer has its home in the stratosphere, beyond which I get so thin that there's only space.

Atmosphere

The Kármán line marks the boundary of the Atmosphere (62 mi. or 100 km).

● Most abundant gas: nitrogen (78%)
● Most important gas for us: oxygen (21%)
● Thickest layer: exosphere (5,600 mi.)

# Front

## Weather Gang

- A splitter who divides streams of air in the Atmosphere
- Changing Weather usually marks this fellow's arrival
- With lots of Front, this guy is often seen on TV weather maps

Front

I'm a highflier who always takes Weather with me. I separate huge masses of air of different density and temperature. As I soar over Earth's surface, the switch between bodies of air stirs up Weather. I come in two flavors: warm and cold. The first is led by a body of warm air pushing back a colder block of air. The second happens in reverse. If one Front catches another, it gets stormy.

- Cold Front symbol: blue line/triangles
- Warm Front symbol: red line/semicircles
- Discovered by: V. and J. Bjerknes

Occluded Fronts happen when a warm Front meets a cold Front.

# Seasons

## ■ Weather Gang

☀ Four of a kind, but never in the same place at the same time
☀ Follow one another in an endless cycle, but not in the Tropics
☀ Caused by Earth's tilted axis (compared with the Sun's axis)

We are the fantastic four: spectacular spring, super summer, awesome autumn (or fall), and wonderful winter. We live life at full tilt, filling the year with our different personalities, one after another, period after period.

The world is tilted at a rakish angle (about 23.5°) as it orbits the Sun. This means that for half the year the Northern Hemisphere leans toward the Sun, and then the Southern Hemisphere nods at the Sun for the rest of the year. The long, happy days of super summer are the days spent leaning toward the Sun. Closer to Equator, Earth receives a steadier dose from the Sun, so the effect of the planet's tilting movement is felt less strongly. There, at Earth's waist, our foursome is replaced by a dynamic duo: the rainy and dry Seasons.

The Arctic and Antarctica each enjoy 24 hours of Sunshine in the summer.

● First day of summer in the U.S.: June 21
● First day of winter in the U.S.: Dec. 21
● First day of summer in Australia: Jan. 1

# Seasons

# Sunshine

## ■ Weather Gang

✴ This lovable, bright character is easy to warm up to
✴ It brings rays of heat and light to planet Earth through space
✴ Its radiating energy is vital to plants and many living things

Bursting with natural warmth and a glowing complexion, I bring a smile to people's faces. It takes me just over eight minutes to travel the 93-million-mile (150-million-km) distance to Earth. Everyone seems to like me when I'm out. What can I say? I'm a popular guy. With my vitamin D–giving rays (the stuff that makes you healthy and feel happy), a small dose of me is sure to brighten you up. But don't go exposing your skin for too long, because my darts of ultraviolet can also be very harmful.

I team up with Water, and together we are the most important things to Life. I warm Earth and give it light. Plants capture my energy and convert it into food in a wonderful process called photosynthesis. In turn, animals feed on this tasty grub. It's all part of the Food Web.

Each Pole has 126 days of continuous Sunshine every year.

● World's sunniest place: Yuma, Arizona
● Hours of Sunshine a year in Yuma: 4,000
● Minimum time to damage skin: 15 min.

Sunshine

# Water Cycle
## ■ Weather Gang

✳ A well-rounded character who never stops recycling
✳ Driven by Sunshine and tied to Precipitation
✳ Made possible 'cause air can soak up and release Water vapor

Stuck on repeat, I have no beginning and no end. With the limited amount of Water on Earth, I've got no choice but to stay on a permanent loop. I rise from any wet surface into the Atmosphere, fall down onto land, and then run back into the Ocean again. I'm the watery wheel that stirs Earth's living shell, keeping it moist and fresh.

At my heart are four processes. Evaporation (where the Sun's energy vaporizes liquid Water) sends Water vapor into the air. Condensation cools this vapor and turns it into droplets, and side by side these molecules form my big, Cloudy face. Precipitation—the splish-splash of rain, hail, sleet, or snow—drops when Clouds can hold no more. Collection of this Water is the final step in my cycle, before I roll on again, again, and again.

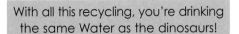
With all this recycling, you're drinking the same Water as the dinosaurs!

● Years Water molecule in Ocean: 3,200
● Months Water molecule in River: 4
● Days Water molecule in Atmosphere: 9

# Water Cycle

# Precipitation

## Weather Gang

- ✳ Moisture that falls from the sky as rain, hail, sleet, or snow
- ✳ One of the vital guys as far as Weather is concerned
- ✳ A skydiver who pitter-patters and performs wonders for Life

Get your umbrella out! Run for cover! It's true that I may spoil a barbecue or trip to the beach, but without my drizzly droplets, all plants and animals would die of thirst. With empty reservoirs, you'd be pretty stinky, too. It's easy to see what my nonappearance does to Life. Next time you are caught in one of my showers, count yourself lucky!

I have four teams of parachuters, each with its own unique outfit. There is common rain that drops in its silky suit; hard-nut hail that plummets and peppers; slow snow that flakes and drifts; and sneezy sleet that mixes rain and snow in a dribble-drabble mess. Fog, mist, and haze don't fall, so they have nothing to do with me, but if I just stay as water vapor and get Atmosphere steamy, I'm called humidity.

Rain falls on average at 30 ft./s (9m/s) and snow at 3 ft./s (1m/s).

- ● Total per year: 5.52 thousand trillion tons
- ● Annual record: Cherrapunji, India, 450 in.
- ● Most rain in one day: Réunion island, 1966

# Precipitation

# Cloud

## ▪ Weather Gang

- ✳ A floating bag of gloom . . . with a silver lining
- ✳ Carries Water vapor around the sky, blown by Wind
- ✳ It might look solid, but you can fly right through it

Gracing the sky like a floating ball of cotton candy, I give the impression of being all soft and fluffy. But plunk your head down on one of my pillows, and you'd get a soggy surprise. My ability to reflect sunlight makes me look whitish, but in reality I'm a dark, wet collection of Water droplets.

I form in the lowest level of Atmosphere as warm air rises. Warm air holds lots of Water vapor at low levels, but as it gets higher and cooler, the vapor condenses. Water droplets are small enough to stay suspended in the air for a while but fall when they get heavy enough. Depending on how I form, I can throw a bewildering variety of shapes: cirrus (high, icy, and wispy), cumulus (fluffy and white), cumulonimbus (fluffy and dark), nimbostratus (thick, dark, and low), and stratus (thin, flat, and low).

Hail inside cumulonimbus Clouds can rip through an aircraft's body.

- ● Thickest: cumulonimbus (up to 65,000 ft.)
- ● Highest: polar mesopheric (up to 53 mi.)
- ● Rain-bearing Cloud: nimbus

Cloud

# Wind

## ■ Weather Gang

✴ Movement of gas in the Atmosphere
✴ Driven by pressure differences in the Atmosphere
✴ Full of bluster, it likes to stir things up

Blow me down! I am simply a natural movement of gas, a breath of fresh air that will give you goose bumps when you feel me fluttering at your drawers! The direction I travel from is one of my defining characteristics (north, east, south, west), and when I occur frequently in the same direction, I'm known as a prevailing Wind.

Because I perform well under pressure, you'll find that I always blow from areas of high pressure to areas of low pressure. The closer these areas are to one another, the greater the difference in air pressure and the faster I blow. On a sunny day, I'm likely to cool things down pleasantly, but when I whip up to gale-force speeds (39–46 mph or 63–74 km/h), I can unroot mighty trees and toss ships around in the Ocean. Life's a total breeze for me!

The fastest recorded Wind was inside a tornado in Oklahoma in 1999.

● Fastest recorded: 318 mph
● Fastest recorded at sea level: 207 mph
● Annual tornado count in U.S.: over 1,000

Wind

# Hurricane
## ■ Weather Gang

* A rotating storm system with a riotous, bad attitude
* Seen in the Northern Hemisphere from July until October
* Appears south of Equator between November and March

A real blowhard, I'm an ill Wind who blows no one any good. It's no use trying to stand up against my violent forces. Wind blusters around, proud of his fierce gales, but he's got nothing on me. I toss mobile homes and cars around like matchsticks, rip up trees, and flatten buildings. Some say "batten down the hatches," but if you see me coming your way, I recommend you skedaddle!

I have my very own Season in the Tropics. I form offshore, fed by Water that evaporates from the Oceans, and stir up the waves before I march onto land to vent my wrath. The Caribbean faces me every year, but meteorologists have become good at predicting where I might land. I'm called "typhoon" in the Pacific and "cyclone" in the Indian Ocean, but I think "psycho" would suit me better!

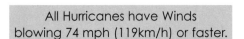

All Hurricanes have Winds blowing 74 mph (119km/h) or faster.

● Deadliest: Bhola cyclone (1970)
● Costliest: Hurricane Katrina (2005)
● Largest: Typhoon Tip (1,348 mi. across)

# Hurricane

# Drought

## ◼ Weather Gang

- ✴ As Water runs out, this guy walks through the door
- ✴ Dusty fellow who is drowned out when Precipitation arrives
- ✴ Never welcome, he spells hardship for everyone he meets

All dry and crackly, I don't expect a great reception. You see, I make life hard for plants, animals, and people by depriving them of Water. Without this liquid, I cause things to shrivel up and suffer. When I hang around for too long, things get worse—I start famines and people starve to death. You'll wish for Precipitation to put an end to my uncontrollable long, hot days.

Drought

The longest Drought lasted 400 years in the Atacama Desert, Chile.

- ● Deadliest: China (1876–1879)
- ● Costliest: Australia (1982), $6 billion
- ● Famous U.S. Drought: Dust Bowl (1930s)

# Flood

## Weather Gang

* Occurs when seas drown coastal areas or Rivers burst their banks
* Spreads out across flat areas called floodplains
* Leaves behind a mess and can become a natural disaster

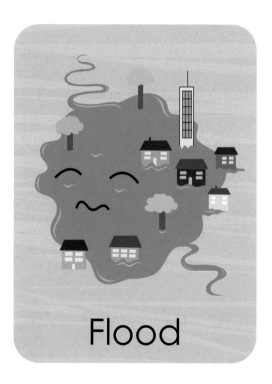
Flood

Break out the sandbags, 'cause here I come! I am a regular visitor to some parts of the world. The Amazon River breaks its banks every year, allowing me to sweep through a vast area of forest. I was once part of the life cycle along the Nile, and the silt and sediment I left behind fertilized its floodplains. As Climate Change gets more heavy handed, you'll be seeing more of me.

- Deadliest: Yellow River, China (1931)
- Costliest: Russia (1991), $60 billion
- Biggest: Amazon (covers 135,140 sq. mi.)

When a Flood happens rapidly with little warning, it's called a flash flood.

# El Niño

## ■ Weather Gang

☀ A mischievous scamp who affects Earth's Climate
☀ Changes Water movement in the Pacific every four years or so
☀ His name is Spanish and means "the little boy"

As a tricky character, always up for a laugh, I mess around with currents in the Pacific Ocean and affect Weather all over the globe. I might be a bit of a kid at heart, but after Seasons, I have the largest impact on the Climate. Even now, global warming gets blamed for the havoc I wreak. Oh, I do love getting away with stuff like that.

By switching the direction of currents in the Pacific Ocean (close to Peru), I cause drier-than-normal Weather in the east and wetter conditions in the west. Atmosphere spreads these changes worldwide and affects people's local Weather. I've been playing hide-and-seek for ages, but that game is almost up. Meteorologists are beginning to understand my global effects. I might not be the wild-card whippersnapper for much longer.

The Pacific Ocean heats up by 9°F (5°C) before El Niño strikes.

● Age: at least 15,000 years
● First recorded by : Captain Carrillo, 1892
● Began to be studied: 1970s

El Niño

# Greenhouse Effect

## ▪ Weather Gang

- ☀ A gassy boy who stops Sun's energy from escaping into space
- ☀ Caused by certain gases in the Atmosphere, especially $CO_2$
- ☀ People get very hot under the collar talking about him

Nobody ever has anything good to say about me. As the cause of global warming, I'm blamed for raising the temperature of the planet. Admittedly, I'm a natural phenomenon, but those in glass houses shouldn't throw stones. My hothouse antics are just as much the fault of you stupid humans! Your crazy love of cars, airplanes, manufacturing, and burning of Fossil Fuels has made my transparent coat so thick that I'm like a giant quilted jacket.

The gases let loose in the Atmosphere act like the glass walls of a greenhouse, trapping heat from the Sun. The worst of these is carbon dioxide ($CO_2$). My coat is slowly but surely causing the Atmosphere to heat up, changing the planet's Climates and melting Earth's frozen Icecaps. Better stop burning so much stuff, eh?

By 2100, climatologists predict the temperature to rise by 2.5–10.4°F.

- ● Discovered by: Joseph Fourier, 1824
- ● Rise in $CO_2$ level since 1860: 40%
- ● Rise in temperature since 1900: 1.5°F

# Greenhouse Effect

# Climate Change

## Weather Gang

- A guy with a bad rep for fiddling with the world's Climate
- Has the power to make the Climate hotter or colder
- Linked to, but not the same as, global warming

I'm a wrench that fouls up the works—a global goblin who's gearing up. I take an impish delight in turning things on their head. A long-term player in the Weather game, I amuse myself by causing lots of problems. I'm changing Earth's "expected weather" patterns, topping off the oceans, warming the planet, changing ecosystems, and taking Weather to new extremes.

Like all the best crime bosses, I have my stooges. All over the world, humans are doing my dirty work for me. Your pollution and increased $CO_2$ production are feeding my friend Greenhouse Effect and causing the world's average temperature to rise. This is global warming. It's normal for me to come and go as part of the planet's natural system, but this is going to be a very lively century for me.

By 2100, climatologists predict the sea level to rise by 31 in. (80 cm).

- Term first coined: start of 20th century
- Rise of sea level: 0.126 in. per year
- Severe water shortage: S.E. Australia

## Climate Change

# CHAPTER 6

Lively Crew

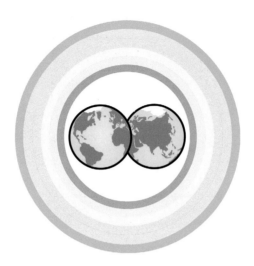

Most planets are nice and clean, but Earth is infested!
A huge number of different Life forms crawl and slither
over its surface. They have invaded every nook and
cranny, from the highest Mountain Ranges to the deepest
Ocean trenches. So that they can survive in specific
regions, these Life forms have evolved into fully equipped
communities (called Biomes), each with its own delicate
mix of plant and animal life. It is these friendly and
sometimes forbidding Biomes that help explain the living
world and make up most of the Lively Crew.

Life

Food Web

Biome

Tundra

Taiga

Temperate Forest

Grassland

Desert

Tropical Rainforest

Open Ocean

Deep Sea

Coral Reef

Conservation

# Life

## ■ Lively Crew

- ☀ A sparky character found in each and every one of us
- ☀ Delicate nature has hung around for billions of years
- ☀ Scientists scan the universe for signs of this guy

I am the mysterious quality that separates lamb from lamb chop—a strong yet delicate force that animates matter and makes you tick. Scientists struggle to capture my spark, but I am a slippery customer who has revealed only some of my secrets. On Earth, I can be found in animals, plants, fungi, bacteria, and other oozing slimes. Although these things are very different, all are carbon- and Water-based beings that are built out of repeating patterns of cells.

Get a load of my unique features. I allow living things to take energy from outside themselves and use it to grow; to adapt to changes in the environment; and to reproduce (make copies of themselves). So far, despite scientists' best efforts to find me elsewhere, I am known only on Earth.

Sea organisms called heterotrophs were the first Life on Earth.

- ● First Life on Earth: 3.8 billion years ago
- ● First animals: 720 million years ago
- ● First people: 200,000 years ago

Life

# Food Web
## ■ Lively Crew

* ☀ A fact of Life that tangles animals and plants in its threads
* ☀ This guzzler exists because it's obsessed with eating
* ☀ Has many different faces—one for every ecosystem

I am the planet's biggest foodie, and I keep tabs on exactly who's filling their stomachs with whom and what. The complex webs I spin connect animals and plants and are impossible to escape from—every living thing, including you, is caught up in them. These interconnected paths show how animals and plants in an area interact or, more straightforwardly, who runs away from whom.

I get pretty complicated pretty quickly, so another way of looking at me is to say that I show how energy moves around in any environment. The solid base of every one of my networks, in every Biome, is plants. These fine fellows take in the Sun's energy to make their food and ultimately provide energy and food for the entire living world. Maybe you are what you eat, but I am what *everyone* eats!

V. Summerhayes and C. Elton published the first example in 1923.

● Individual path called: food chain
● Term for plants: producers
● Term for herbivores: primary consumers

# Food Web

# Biome

## ■ Lively Crew

✴ Acts as a big umbrella that ecosystems gather under
✴ Has several different forms, from Deep Sea to Desert
✴ Animals and plants survive by adapting to its conditions

We may be a posse of shy and retiring planet lovers, but we're hardly a meek bunch. We Biomes are earthy characters who divide and conquer. Between us, we have every inch of land and every cubic foot of fresh water and salt water covered.

We are also sometimes known as ecosystems (all the plants, animals, and type of terrain in any area), but there is a small yet important difference. We Biomes are a way to classify similar types of ecosystems around the world. Desert Biome, for example, includes the Arizona desert ecosystem in the U.S., as well as the Sahara ecosystem in Africa. We depend mostly on Climate and Latitude, so our global map looks a bit like the world is wearing a multicolored, striped sweater!

Biomes of the Cape Floral Region, South Africa, have 9,000 plant species.

● Term *biome* coined by F. Clements, 1916
● Term *ecosystem* coined: 1936
● Largest land Biome: tundra

Biome

# Tundra

## ■ Lively Crew

✳ The original Mr. Frosty, he knows all about life in a cold Climate
✳ Found high in mountains and hugging the edges of Icecaps
✳ Characterized by short plants and very brief summers

Ice cool, I am the world's coldest Biome. You can find me in Arctic and alpine areas (above the timberline). Very little can grow because high Winds and chilly temperatures mean any trees that are bold enough to try are forced to grow along the ground. The soil is frozen solid in my Arctic areas. This makes the growing season a mere 50 to 60 days each year.

Tundra

Tundra has 1.1 trillion tons of carbon frozen in its permafrost soil.

● Average annual temperature: −14.8°F
● Precipitation: 6–10 in. per year
● Coverage: about 20% of Earth's land

# Taiga
## Lively Crew ■

* This guy's thick "fir" coat of trees is well adapted to the cold
* Restricted to the Northern Hemisphere, south of the Arctic Tundra
* A Biome that sometimes goes by another name—boreal forest

Taiga

I'm a northern man who dresses in fir (trees). Home to some of the world's inaccessible wildernesses, I contain Earth's most northerly forests and about one-third of all its trees. My gritty conifers are survivors. Their branches slope down to help the snow slide off them, and their leaves are hard-wearing needles with a waxy outer layer. They can last all winter, even with the ground frozen solid.

● Average annual temperature: 30°F
● Precipitation: below 39 in. per year
● Coverage: about 17% of Earth's land

Taiga has the fewest animal and plant species of any Biome.

# Temperate Forest

## ▪ Lively Crew

✴ This woody character likes life on the mild side
✴ Changes color in the fall as trees start to lose their leaves
✴ It's losing out to farmland, particularly in Europe

Everything in moderation is my motto. I am a polite and restrained fellow, and I go quietly and modestly about my business—going to great extremes is not for this Biome. I'll leave that to the likes of Tundra and Taiga! Climate is totally temperate in my regions.

I am generally found directly south of Taiga, in parts of North America, Europe, and northeast Asia. My Weather is much balmier, though. I won't stand for long, cold winters, and my summers are longer and warmer than those in the chilly wastes of Taiga. I allow myself one emotional moment per year. Every autumn, as the Weather cools, my broad-leaved trees perform a magnificent change of color before they drop their leaves in a grandiose display . . . that leaves me naked!

It's home to the giant redwood tree, the tallest in the world.

● Average annual temperature: 50°F
● Precipitation: 30–60 in. per year
● Coverage: unknown (greatly reduced)

# Temperate Forest

# Grassland
## ■ Lively Crew

- ☀ This free-range Biome loves wide-open spaces
- ☀ Likes it dry, but not too dry—a little rain is good
- ☀ Also known as prairie, Pampas, savanna, veld, and steppe

I am the character with a hundred names—a "steppe" above the rest. Wherever I am found in the world, my Biome is given a different moniker. There are many of me on Earth. I roll out across Continents like an enormous carpet, but I'm an in-betweener, a piggy in the middle, forever stuck between Desert and forest. Not enough rain falls for many trees to grow, but grasses and smaller plants seem to love me to pieces!

I have two main types. Temperate Grassland almost always lacks trees and is found in places with temperate Climates, such as Argentina and southern Russia. Savanna is found in warmer parts of the world, such as Africa. It has scattered trees, but not enough for forests to form. As with many Biomes, farmland is taking me over.

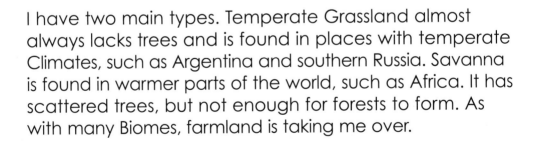

Grasslands once covered half of Africa.

- ● Average annual temperature: 50°C
- ● Precipitation: 10–60 in. per year
- ● Height of tallest grasses: 6.5 ft.

Grassland

# Desert
## ■ Lively Crew

- ☀ It's safe to say this guy has a pretty bleak outlook
- ☀ Made of sand, Rock, or gravel, he is always dry
- ☀ A big Biome where Life exists right on the edge

Stay far away if you value your life. I am a dangerous biome with a lethal track record when it comes to humans. That's because you're wet, soppy things, and I am dryness personified. My regions include the world's most dusty and arid places. Some of them have seen nary a drop of precipitation for years. Feeling thirsty yet?

I can be served either hot or cold. Hot Deserts are mostly found fairly close to the Equator. Cold ones, such as Asia's Gobi Desert, are closer to the Poles. Although I'm a place humans dread, amazingly I'm not barren of Life. Some plants and animals have adapted to my harsh conditions extremely well. Many reptiles are at home in hot Deserts. Their ability to go for long periods without food and to survive on very little Water means I suit them very well.

The Sahara, North Africa, is the largest hot desert, at 3.5 million sq. mi.

- ● Average temp. (hot Deserts): 73°F
- ● Precipitation: about 10 in. per year
- ● Coverage: 20% of Earth's land

Desert

# Tropical Rainforest

## ■ Lively Crew

☀ A fulsome and fruity character, bursting with flavor
☀ Releasing water vapor and storing $CO_2$, it's Earth's life belt
☀ Veers from wet to steamy and then back to wet again

A riot of wild colors and wilder creatures, I'm home to more species of animals and plants than any other Biome! My welcoming nature comes from my tropical temperament. It's almost constantly warm and wet within my bounds, so trees and plants can flower and fruit at pretty much any time. I'm crawling with insect life . . . and every other kind—right up to the bigger, more attention-grabbing animals like anacondas and tigers.

I don't experience Seasons like most other land biomes. Yes, I have a "dry season," but it's still very, very wet. I don't deal in drizzle, showers, or any of that nonsense. When it rains, it rains—real rain with cloudbursts, thunder, and everything. Sadly, nowadays I am under attack. People want my trees for timber and my land for farms.

In two centuries, its coverage has dropped from 14% to 6% of Earth.

● Average annual temperature: 73°F
● Precipitation: more than 78 in. per year
● Coverage: currently 3.4 million sq. mi.

# Tropical Rainforest

# Open Ocean

✳ A vast Biome of endless open Water
✳ A mysterious character who is always far away from land
✳ Home to speed merchants, drifters, and the world's top divers

I am the Big Blue. You'd better believe it, baby! I'm the biggest and the best. Water covers almost three-fourths of Earth's surface, and most of it is Open Ocean. My regions include all seawater above the Deep Sea and outside the coastal zones. In many ways though, I'm like a wet Desert, home to just a pitiful tenth of Earth's marine species.

Many of the creatures that live within me inhabit my sunlit Waters near the surface. This is also the hangout of phytoplankton (say "fie-toe-plank-ton"). Like plants, these microscopic algae and other tiny beasties have the ability to harness the Sun's energy to make food. They make oxygen as a byproduct. Phytoplankton produce as much oxygen as all the plants on land put together.

Point Nemo (Pacific Ocean) is the farthest point from land, at 1,670 mi.

● Largest inhabitant: blue whale
● Fastest inhabitant: cosmopolitan sailfish
● An Ocean scientist is an oceanologist

# Open Ocean

# Deep Sea

## ■ Lively Crew

* ☀ A deeply dippy but deathly dark Biome
* ☀ Full of hidden depths, this dark fellow is still largely unexplored
* ☀ Home to weird creatures, with more discovered every year

I'm totally deep, man. Yeah. I'm the deepest there is—the Biome that goes way, wa-a-a-a-y down. Lying still and brooding underneath the massive Open Ocean Biome, I'm a man of many, many mysteries.

I'm not just deep—I'm dark. Way dark. Darker than you can imagine. The force of all the Water pressing down from above makes pressures intense. Life does not appreciate all these hardships, but I do play host to a scrap of Life . . . I'm a place where odd beasts hunt and scavenge to survive. Bits of dead fish and other stuff drift down into my depths as a kind of "marine snow" and settle on the bottom. Some creatures root around in it, scavenging for food. Others seek out these rubbish junkies and eat them. That's the way it is in the deep zone.

Many Deep Sea fish emit their own light (called bioluminescence).

● Depth Deep Sea begins: 3,300 ft.
● Deepest Ocean: Pacific (ave. 12,900 ft.)
● Average temperature: 37°F

Deep Sea

# Coral Reef
## ■ Lively Crew

☀ This tropical Biome is a favorite with scuba divers
☀ Coral is formed from the exoskeletons of living creatures
☀ It might be shallow, but there's no arguing that it is bright

I'm a submarine beauty, a little ray of sunshine called Coral. I like blue skies, the Sun, warm seas, fish, and bright colors. I'm the Biome where the Ocean comes out to play! My tropical paradise of shallow Water is home to the most incredible displays of sea life.

Please don't think I'm superficial just because my waters aren't deep. The complicated relationships in my busy ecosystems have taken great minds many years to figure out . . . although studying in my balmy waters isn't what most people call hard work! Some people call my group the rainforests of the sea. In a way, they're right. I'm home to more species than any other ecosystem in the ocean. I'm a delicate flower, though, and humans are damaging me with pollution and by overharvesting my fish.

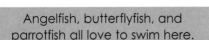

Angelfish, butterflyfish, and parrotfish all love to swim here.

● Largest: Great Barrier Reef, Australia
● Most common in: Indo-Pacific region
● Coverage: 109,800 sq. mi.

# Coral Reef

# Conservation

## ■ Lively Crew

✹ This caring character does its best to protect the natural world
✹ Fights those who plunder nature and threaten Earth's future
✹ Loves its work, but wishes that it didn't need to be done

Some people spend like there's no tomorrow. My mission in life is to save. It's not money I'm interested in saving, though, it's nature. Like a green superhero, I want to preserve the animals, plants, and wild places of the world.

You might think that my job sounds like a piece of cake. Nature does pretty well when left to its own devices, so what's the problem? Well, all sorts of people want a piece of nature, for all sorts of reasons. Some want to take her land for farming or open it up with mines. Others want what she grows—her trees for timber or her animals for food. The upshot is that I've got my work cut out for me. There are lots of reasons why I do this job. I want to preserve as much of nature's beauty as possible, for future generations to enjoy. It's a labor of love. Maybe you'll help me out, too!

WWF is the largest Conservation organization (over 5 million members).

● First national park: Yellowstone (U.S.)
● Largest national park: N.E. Greenland
● World Wildlife Fund (WWF) started: 1961

Conservation

# INDEX

# GLOSSARY

**Air pressure** Pressure on the ground exerted by the weight of the atmosphere above.

**Algae** Simple plantlike organisms. Many algae are single-celled, but seaweeds are made up of many cells.

**Atmosphere** The layer of air that surrounds Earth. Beyond the atmosphere is space.

**Biosphere** The parts of Earth occupied by living organisms, namely its crust and atmosphere.

**Climate zone** A section of Earth's surface where the climate is roughly the same throughout the zone.

**$CO_2$** Carbon dioxide—a gas that occurs naturally in the atmosphere and is also formed when things are burned.

**Condensation** Droplets of water that form on surfaces as a result of water vapor turning to a liquid.

**Convection forces** Forces created by the movement of heat through a liquid or semiliquid material.

**Ecosystem** A biological community made up of living organisms and their surrounding environment.

**Environment** Natural surroundings in which humans, animals, and plants develop and grow during their lives.

**Equinox** One of the two days of the year (March 21 and September 23) when day and night are of equal length.

**Estuary** A section of a river, near its mouth, that is affected by the tide. In an estuary, fresh water and seawater mix.

**Evaporation** The changing of liquid into gas—for example, the changing of water into water vapor.

**Fjord** A long, deep coastal inlet, formed when glacial valleys were flooded by the sea after the last Ice Age.

**Food chain** A series of living things, each dependent on the next for food. An example is grass–wildebeest–lion.

**Geyser** A natural fountain where water heated underground shoots up through Earth's surface.

**Global warming** A general warming of Earth's atmosphere caused by pollution from greenhouse gases.

**Hemisphere** Literally "half a sphere." Geographers split Earth into two hemispheres: the Northern Hemisphere (north of the equator) and the Southern (south of it).

**Humidity** The level of water vapor in the surrounding air. Air is humid if the level of water vapor in it is high.

**Lava** Molten rock that has poured from a volcano or fissure out onto the surface of Earth.

**Magma** Molten rock that lies beneath Earth's surface.

**Metal** A chemical element that conducts heat and electricity well, such as gold, silver, or iron, or an alloy (mixture) of these elements—for example, bronze.

**Monsoon** A wind that blows across the Indian subcontinent and other parts of southern Asia at roughly the same time every year. It brings the rainy season.

**Moon** A massive body in space that orbits (travels around) a planet. Earth has one moon; some planets have several.

**Ore** Rock that can be heated or otherwise treated to yield metal or other valuable minerals.

# GLOSSARY

**Organism** A living thing. Plants, animals, fungi, and algae are all types of organisms.

**Ozone layer** A thin layer in the atmosphere, made up largely of ozone, that absorbs most of the ultraviolet radiation in sunlight.

**Photosynthesis** The process by which plants and algae use sunlight to turn carbon dioxide and water into food.

**Phytoplankton** Plankton (small organisms that live in water) that create their own food by photosynthesis. They drift with the ocean currents.

**Plate tectonics** The movement of the various plates of Earth's surface.

**Richter scale** A scale measuring the relative size and power of earthquakes.

**Sea level** The altitude (height of land) that corresponds to the average surface level of the sea. Some places on land, such as Death Valley in California, are below sea level.

**Solar system** The Sun and the planets and other bodies that orbit it, including Earth.

**Solstice** Either of the two days of the year when the Sun is farthest from the equator. The summer solstice is the longest day, and the winter solstice is the shortest.

**Ultraviolet** Light radiation with a wavelength just shorter than that of visible light.

**Water vapor** Droplets of water suspended in air.